Complete Smoothie & Juicing Recipes Cookbook for Beginners

David Marco

Table of Contents

Cumber Melon Smoothie

Prep/Total Time: 15 min

Ingredients

- 2 cups less-fat plain Greek yogurt
- 1/3 cup nectar
- 3 cups cleaved honeydew melon
- 2 medium cucumbers
- 1 to 2 tablespoons new mint leaves
- 2 cups squashed ice solid shapes

Procedure

1. Place half of every one of the accompanying in a blender like yogurt, nectar, melon, cucumber, and, whenever wanted, mint blending and mixing. Add 1 cup ice cover and interaction until smooth and afterward fill three glasses. At long last rehash with residual fixings

Triple Berry Smoothie

Total Time: 5 Min

Ingredients

- 1 banana, frozen
- 1 cup milk
- ½ cup Greek yogurt
- ½ cup blueberries, frozen
- ¼ cup strawberries, frozen
- ¼ cup raspberries, froze

Procedure

1. all fixings place in a blender and afterward blending .
2. Mixing proceed until smooth, adding more fluid as your required

Alan's Going Green Smoothie

Total Time:
11 Minutes

Ingredients

- 240 ml water
- 2 cups green grapes
- 2 cuts pineapple, stripped, divided
- 1 medium bananas, stripped
- 2 medium limes, stripped
- ½ cup cashews, simmered, unsalted
- 2 jalapeño, stemmed, cultivated
- 4 cups new spinach
- 2 cups ice blocks

Procedure

1. All fixings Place in the Vitamix holder in the request recorded and secure the cover.
2. Initially, Start the blender with the least speed and afterward rapidly increment it to its most elevated speed
3. At last, mix for 1 moment or until the ideal consistency is reached, and afterward utilizing the alter to squeeze fixings toward the edges.

4 Key Lime Kiwi Smoothie

Total Time:
10 Minutes
Ingredients

- 120 ml water
- 1 lime, stripped
- 4 (280 g) medium kiwis
- 2 (400 g) enormous pear, divided, cultivated
- 6 pitted dates, ¼ cup nectar,
- 2 cups ice blocks

Procedure

1. With a peeler or paring blade, eliminate the strip and white essence from the lime and afterward, leaving simply the tissue.
2. All fixings place into the Vitamix holder in the request recorded and secure the top.
3. Initially, start the blender at its slowest speed, then, at that point, increment with the most noteworthy speed.
4. Mix for 30 seconds and afterward utilizing the alter to squeeze fixings toward the edges

Just Peachy Smoothie

Total Time:
11 Minutes

Ingredients

- 1 cup red grapes, or green grapes
- 2 cups new blueberries
- 2 peaches, pitted, split
- 2 cups ice 3D squares

Procedure

1. All fixings Place into the Vitamix compartment in the request recorded and secure cover.
2. Right off the bat, Start the blender on its most minimal speed and afterward speed up.
3. At long last, mix for 40-45 seconds as required

Good Morning Green Smoothie

Total:

5 mins

Ingredients

- 1 cup unsweetened soy milk
- 1 cup new spinach
- 1 Persian (smaller than usual) cucumber, generally slashed (1 cup)
- 1 cup generally hacked Granny Smith apple
- 1 ½ cups frozen pineapple pieces
- 2 Tbsp hemp seeds
- Pinch of kosher salt
- 1 Tbsp agave nectar

Procedure

1. Spot all fixings in a blender, beginning with hemp milk. Mixing until smooth, around 1 moment.

7 Almond Yogurt, Peach and Banana Smoothie

Total Time:
11 Minutes

Ingredients

- 1 cup almond milk
- ½ cup vanilla almond yogurt
- ¼ Tbsp ground turmeric
- 2 pieces ginger root, 1/8" cuts
- 1 cup frozen peach cuts
- 1 cup frozen banana, cuts

Procedure

1. Initially, all fixings place into the Vitamix holder and secure the cover.
2. Start the blender with the most reduced speed and afterward speed up.
3. At long last brief mixing and utilizing the alter to squeeze fixings toward the cutting edges.

8 Autumn Sweet Potato Smoothie

Total Time:
11 Minutes

Ingredients

- 2⅔ cup red grapes
- 1 medium orange, stripped, zested
- 1 yam, stripped, cooked
- 1 medium apple, cultivated
- 1 piece new ginger root, ½" cut
- 4 medjool dates, pitted
- ½ cup frozen cranberries
- 4 cups ice blocks

Procedure

1. Initially, all fixings place into the Vitamix holder and secure the cover.
2. Start the blender with the most minimal speed and afterward increment blender the most elevated speed.
3. At long last 45 second mixing and utilizing the alter to squeeze fixings toward the edges.

9 Pomegranate Beet Smoothie

Total Time:
10 Minutes

Ingredients

- ½ cup ice 3D squares
- ½ little beet
- 2 Tbsp new parsley leaves
- ⅓ cup spinach
- 1 piece ginger root, 1/4" cut
- ½ orange, stripped, split
- ¼ lemon, stripped
- ½ cup pomegranate juice

Procedure

1. All fixings place into the Vitamix compartment in the request recorded and secure the sharp edge base.
2. Start the blender with the least speed and afterward increment the blender to the most elevated speed.
3. At last, 45 second mixing

10 Papaya Vanilla Smoothie

Total Time:
10 Minutes

Ingredients

- 1/4 cups papaya, stripped, cultivated
- ½ little banana, stripped
- 1 cut pineapple, stripped, divided around 1/2 inch thick
- 1 cup new spinach
- 1 scoop protein powder, or almonds or cashews
- 1 cup ice solid shapes

Procedure

1. All ingredients mixing together and place into the Vitamix container in the order listed and then secure the lid.
2. First, start the blender with the lowest speed and then increase the blender with the highest speed, using the tamper to press ingredients toward the blades for well blending.
3. Finally, blend for 45 seconds.

11 Nuts and Grains Breakfast Smoothie

Total Time:
10 Minutes

Ingredients

- 720 ml alternative milk
- 3 medium bananas, peeled, halved
- 3 Tbsp peanut butter
- 5 pitted dates
- 3 Tbsp rolled oats
- 1 cup ice cubes

Procedure

1. All fixings combining as one and spot into the Vitamix compartment in the request recorded and afterward secure the top.
2. In the first place, start the blender with the least speed and afterward increment the blender with the most noteworthy speed, utilizing the alter to squeeze fixings toward the sharp edges for well mixing.
3. At last, mix for 45 seconds.

12 Blackberry Beet Smoothie Bowl

Total Time:
10 Minutes

Ingredients

- 1/2 cups almond yogurt
- 2 cups blackberries
- 1 (110 g) beet, cooked
- 1 cup new spinach
- 1 cup frozen peach cuts
- 1 cup frozen mango lumps
- 2 Tbsp chia seeds
- 1 Tbsp nectar, discretionary

Procedure

1. All fixings combining as one and spot into the Vitamix holder in the request recorded and afterward secure the top.
2. In the first place, start the blender with the most minimal speed and afterward increment the blender with the most noteworthy speed, utilizing the alter to squeeze fixings toward the edges for well mixing.
3. At last, mix for 45 seconds.
4. Segment into bowls and top with your number one fixings, and we love toasted coconut, shaved almonds and new blackberries for this bowl!

13 Superfood Morning Smoothie Bowl

Total Time:
10 Minutes

Ingredients

- 1 Tbsp coconut oil
- 3 Tbsp (45 g) flaxseed oil
- 1/4 cups hemp seeds
- 1 Tbsp matcha green tea powder
- 2 cups mango nectar
- 2 cups frozen mango lumps
- 1 piece new ginger root, 1/4" cut

Procedure

1. All fixings combining as one and spot into the Vitamix holder in the request recorded and afterward secure the cover.
2. In the first place, start the blender with the most minimal speed and afterward increment the blender with the most elevated speed, utilizing the alter to squeeze fixings toward the cutting edges for well mixing.
3. At long last, mix for 30 seconds.

14 Pumpkin Pie Smoothie

Total Time: 5 minute

Ingredients

- 1/2 cup skim milk*
- 2 Tbsp unadulterated maple syrup
- 2/3 cup pumpkin puree
- 1 cup ice 3D shapes
- 1 frozen banana
- 1/2 cup vanilla Greek yogurt*
- 1/4 Tbsp ground cinnamon
- 1/4 Tbsp pumpkin pie spice*

Procedure

1. Take an amazing blender.
2. Every one of the fixings spot to the blender in the request recorded. Mixing with high velocity 3 minutes or until smooth. Pause and scratch down the sides of the blender on a case by case basis.
3. milk to disperse in case it's excessively thick, or add a couple more ice shapes for a thicker surface whenever wanted. Taste, then, at that point add more flavors

15 Warm Apple Ginger Smoothie

Total Time:
12 Minutes

Ingredients

- 1 cup squeezed apple
- 2 (320 g) apples, split, cultivated
- 1 cut lemon, ⅛" thick
- 1 piece new ginger root, ⅛" cut
- ¼ teaspoon pumpkin flavor

Procedure

1. All fixings combining as one and spot into the Vitamix compartment in the request recorded and afterward secure the cover.
2. In the first place, start the blender with the least speed and afterward increment the blender with the most high speed, utilizing the alter to squeeze fixings toward the edges for well mixing.
3. At last, mix for 2 minute .

16 Swirled Fruit and Honey Smoothie

Total Time:
11 Minutes

Ingredients

- 2 teaspoons flax supper
- 1 Tablespoon nectar, discretionary
- 1½ (180 g) frozen banana, stripped, divided
- ⅓ cup (80 ml) oat milk, or elective milk
- 1½ cup (360 ml) vanilla soy yogurt, or low-fat vanilla yogurt

Procedure

1. Clean the container. Milk, vanilla yogurt, flax meal, honey, and frozen banana mixing together and place into the Vitamix container in the order listed and then secure the lid.
2. First, start the blender with the lowest speed and then increase the blender with the highest speed, using the tamper to press ingredients toward the blades for well blending.
3. Finally, blend for 45 seconds.
4. Pour over the combination in the serving glasses and afterward twirling together prior to drinking.

17 Banana Raspberry Green Smoothie

Total Time:
10 Minutes

Ingredients

- 1/2 cups new mint leaves
- 4 (440 g) little bananas, stripped
- 3 cups frozen raspberries
- 2 cups almond milk
- 2 cups new spinach
- 1 cup romaine lettuce

Procedure

1. All fixings combining as one and spot into the Vitamix compartment in the request recorded and afterward secure the top.
2. In the first place, start the blender with the least speed and afterward increment the blender with the highest speed, utilizing the alter to squeeze fixings toward the cutting edges for well mixing.
3. At last, mix for 45 seconds.

18 Cake Batter Smoothie

Total Time:
5 MINUTES

Ingredients

- ⅔ cup milk - more on a case by case basis
- chocolate syrup, sprinkles
- 2 cups ice
- 1 cup plain or vanilla yogurt
- ⅔ cup yellow cake blend - dry

Procedure

1. Add ice, yogurt (or ice cream) cake mix, and milk to a blender
2. Blending continue until smooth and then check consistency,
3. If too thick, add a few tablespoons of milk and Again blending to desired consistency. Serve immediately with chocolate syrup and sprinkles if desired.

19 Invigorating Citrus Carrot Juice

Time
5 minutes

INGREDIENTS:

- water - 1.5 cup
- pineapple - 3 cups
- baby carrots - 1 1/2 cups
- lemon - 1 large, wheel-shaped slice, peel on
- ice - 2 1/2 cups
- ginger - 1 Tbsp

Procedure

1. All fixings combining as one and spot into the Vitamix holder in the request recorded and afterward secure the top.
2. In the first place, start the blender with the most reduced speed and afterward increment the blender with the most noteworthy speed, utilizing the alter to squeeze fixings toward the sharp edges for well mixing.
3. At last, mix for 60-90 seconds.

20 Winter Green Smoothie with Yuzu

Total Time:
10 Minutes

Ingredients

- 3 (450 g) medium apples, quartered, cultivated
- 1 Tablespoon Honey
- 1 (250 g) satsuma mandarin, stripped, split
- ½ (25 g) yuzu, stripped
- 4 cups komatsuna

Procedure

1. All fixings combining as one and spot into the Vitamix compartment in the request recorded and afterward secure the cover.
2. In the first place, start the blender with the least speed and afterward increment the blender with the most elevated speed, utilizing the alter to squeeze fixings toward the sharp edges for well mixing.
3. At last, mix for 50 seconds.

21 Chocolate Avocado Nutella Smoothie

Total Time: 10 minute

Ingredients

- 2 Tbsp hazelnut spread
- 2 Tbsp unsalted almond margarine
- ½ avocado
- 300 ml home-made almond milk
- 3 Tbsp Greek non-fat plain yogurt, non-dairy
- 2 Tbsp chocolate protein powder

Procedure

1. All fixings combining as one and spot into the Vitamix holder in the request recorded and afterward secure the top.
2. In the first place, start the blender with the most minimal speed and afterward increment the blender with the most noteworthy speed, utilizing the alter to squeeze fixings toward the edges for well mixing.
3. At last, mix for 30-60 seconds.

22 Cherry, Pistachio, Cardamom kombucha Smoothie

Total Time:
5 Minutes

Ingredients

- 360 ml fermented tea
- 1 cup frozen peache cuts, cuts (defrosted)
- 2 Tbsp pistachios, shelled
- 1 Tbsp nectar, discretionary
- ½ Tbsp ground cardamom
- ½ frozen banana, stripped, divided
- 1 cup (140 g) frozen cherries

Procedure

1. All fixings combining as one and spot into the Vitamix holder in the request recorded and afterward secure the cover.
2. In the first place, start the blender with the most reduced speed and afterward increment the blender with the most elevated speed, utilizing the alter to squeeze fixings toward the cutting edges for well mixing.

3. At long last, mix for brief 20 seconds.

23 Vegan Chocolate Date Shake

Total Time:
11 Minutes

Ingredients

- 2 Tbsp crude cashews
- 2 Tbsp unsweetened cocoa powder
- ½ cup sans dairy coconut yogurt
- 1½ cup ice solid shapes
- 2 Tbsp Home-made date syrup
- 1 banana, stripped

Procedure

1. All fixings combining as one and spot into the Vitamix holder in the request recorded and afterward secure the top.
2. All fixings submerge the beneath fluids in blender
3. In the first place, start the blender with the most minimal speed and afterward increment the blender with the most noteworthy speed, utilizing the alter to squeeze fixings toward the edges for well mixing.
4. At long last, mix for 60 second.

24 Tropical Yogurt Freeze

Total Time:

10 Minutes

Ingredients

- 1½ cup low-fat vanilla yogurt
- ¾ pound frozen pineapple lumps
- ¾ pound frozen mango lumps

Procedure

1. All fixings combining as one and spot into the Vitamix holder in the request recorded and afterward secure the cover.
2. All fixings drench the underneath fluids in blender
3. In the first place, start the blender with the most reduced speed and afterward increment the blender with the most elevated speed, utilizing the alter to squeeze fixings toward the cutting edges for well mixing. Mix for 45-60 second.
4. In around 30-60 seconds, the sound of the engine will change, and four hills should frame. Stop the

machine. Don't over blend or liquefying will happen. Serve right away.

25 Peach Soy Sherbet

Total Time:
11 Minutes

Ingredients

- 1 Tbsp vanilla concentrate
- 1½ pound frozen peach cuts
- 1½ cup soy milk
- 4 (60 g) nectar, to taste

Procedure

1. All fixings combining as one and spot into the Vitamix compartment in the request recorded and afterward secure the top.
2. All fixings inundate the beneath fluids in blender
3. In the first place, start the blender with the least speed and afterward increment the blender with the most noteworthy speed, utilizing the alter to squeeze fixings toward the sharp edges for well mixing.
4. In around 30-60 seconds, the sound of the engine will change and four hills should frame. Stop the machine. Don't over blend or dissolving will happen. Serve right away.

26 Strawberry Yogurt Freeze

Total Time:
11 Minutes

Ingredients

- 1½ cup almond yogurt
- 1½ pounds frozen strawberries

Procedure

1. All fixings combining as one and spot into the Vitamix holder in the request recorded and afterward secure the cover.
2. All fixings submerge the beneath fluids in blender
3. In the first place, start the blender with the most minimal speed and afterward increment the blender with the most noteworthy speed, utilizing the alter to squeeze fixings toward the cutting edges for well mixing.
4. In around 30-60 seconds, the sound of the engine will change and four hills should frame. Stop the machine. Don't over blend or dissolving will happen. Serve right away.

27 Citrus Carrot Juice

Total Time:
11 Minutes

Ingredients

- 2 cuts lemon, with strip, ¼" cuts
- 2 cups ice 3D squares
- 1 cup water
- 6 (600 g) cuts of pineapple, stripped, with center
- 4 (220 g) medium carrots, washed, split

Procedure

1. All fixings combining as one and spot into the Vitamix compartment in the request recorded and afterward secure the cover.
2. All fixings inundate the underneath fluids in blender
3. In the first place, start the blender with the least speed and afterward increment the blender with the most elevated speed, utilizing the alter to squeeze fixings toward the edges for well mixing. Mix for 60 second.

28 Chocolate Avocado Freeze

Total Time:
10 Minutes

Ingredients

- ⅓ cup Home-made Date Syrup
- 5¾ cup ice fledgling
- 3 (360 g) bananas, stripped, divided
- ¾ (100 g) avocado, hollowed, stripped
- ½ cup unsweetened cocoa powder

Procedure

1. All fixings combining as one and spot into the Vitamix holder in the request recorded and afterward secure the top.
2. All fixings drench the beneath fluids in blender
3. In the first place, start the blender with the most reduced speed and afterward increment the blender with the most high speed, utilizing the alter to squeeze fixings toward the edges for well mixing. Mix for 30 second.
4. In around 30-60 seconds, the sound of the engine will change and four hills should shape. Stop the

machine. Don't over blend or liquefying will happen. Serve right away.

29 Basil Walnut Pesto

TOTAL TIME10 mins

Ingredients

- 3 cloves garlic
- 1/2 cup olive oil
- Salt and newly ground dark pepper
- 2 cups new basil leaves stuffed
- 1 cups new parsley stuffed
- 1/4 cup Parmesan cheddar
- 1/4 cup pecans

Procedure

1. add basil, parsley, Parmesan cheddar, pecans, and garlic. Heartbeat until coarsely cleaved In a blender, around 10 heartbeats.
2. With the engine running, gradually shower in the olive oil and afterward mixing until smooth. salt and pepper add to tast.

30 Whole Fruit Margarita

Total Time:

10 Minutes

Ingredients

- 1 lemon, stripped
- ⅓ cup nectar
- 6 cups ice shapes
- 180 ml tequila
- ½ cup orange alcohol
- 1 medium orange, stripped, zested
- 1 lime, stripped

Procedure

1. With a peeler or paring blade, then, at that point eliminate the strip and white essence from the natural products, leaving simply the tissue.

2. All fixings combining as one and spot into the Vitamix holder in the request recorded and afterward secure the cover.
3. All fixings drench the underneath fluids in blender
4. In the first place, start the blender with the most reduced speed and afterward increment the blender with **high speed**, utilizing the alter to squeeze fixings toward the cutting edges for well mixing. Mix for 30-45 second.

32 Kale and Pear Green Smoothie

Total Time:
11 Minutes

Ingredients

- ½ (90 g) Bartlett pear, cored
- 1 cup kale
- 2 cups ice 3D shapes
- ½ cup water
- 1 cup green grapes
- 1 (130 g) medium orange, stripped, quartered
- 1 (100 g) little banana, stripped

Procedure

1. All fixings combining as one and spot into the Vitamix compartment in the request recorded and afterward secure the cover.
2. All fixings inundate the underneath fluids in blender
3. In the first place, start the blender with the least speed and afterward increment the blender with the

high speed, utilizing the alter to squeeze fixings toward the sharp edges for well mixing. Mix for 45 second.

33 Fresh Tomato Sauce

Total Time:

51 Minutes

Ingredients

- 1.4 kg ready roma tomatoes, divided
- 120 g yellow onion, stripped
- 1 little carrot
- ¼ cup tomato glue
- 2 garlic cloves, stripped
- 2 Tbsp dried basil
- 2 Tbsp dried oregano
- 1 Tbsp genuine salt

Procedure

1. All fixings combining as one and spot into the Vitamix holder in the request recorded and afterward secure the top.
2. All fixings submerge the beneath fluids in blender
3. In the first place, start the blender with the most minimal speed and afterward increment the blender with the high speed, utilizing the alter to squeeze fixings toward the edges for well mixing. Mix for 45 second.
4. Fill pan and stew for 35 to 40 minutes

34 Freshly Minted Berry Smoothie

Total Time:
11 Minutes

Ingredients

- 1 cup kale
- 1 Tbsp new mint leaves
- 1 Tbsp vanilla concentrate
- 2 cups frozen blended berries
- 2 cups almond milk
- 2 (100 g) kiwis, stripped, split
- 2 pitted dates

Procedure

1. All fixings combining as one and spot into the Vitamix compartment in the request recorded and afterward secure the cover.

2. All fixings submerge the underneath fluids in blender
3. In the first place, start the blender with the least speed and afterward increment the blender with the high speed, utilizing the alter to squeeze fixings toward the edges for well mixing. Mix for 60 second.

35 Harvest Cheddar Soup

Total Time:
20 Minutes

Ingredients

- ⅛ Tbsp ground nutmeg
- ⅛ Tbsp ground dark pepper
- ½ Tbsp salt, discretionary
- 1 cup cheddar, destroyed
- 2 cups chicken stock
- 2 Tbsp white wine
- ¼ (40 g) medium onion
- ½ (50 g) celery stem
- 2 (400 g) granny smith apples, cored, split
- 1 (285 g) medium reddish brown potato, cooked
- ⅛ Tbsp dried thyme

Procedure

1. Potatoes,broth, wine, onion, celery, apples thyme, nutmeg, pepper, and salt spot into the Vitamix compartment in the request recorded and secure the cover.

2. In the first place, start the blender with the least speed and afterward increment the blender with the high speed, utilizing the alter to squeeze fixings toward the sharp edges for well mixing. Mix for 5 moment 45 second.
3. Drop in cheddar through the cover plug opening. Mix an aditional 10 seconds.

37 Chicken Potato Spinach Soup

Total Time:
20 Minutes

Ingredients

- 1 cup chicken stock
- 1½ cup milk, or cashew milk
- ½ cup medium onion, stripped
- 3 (415 g) medium chestnut potatoes, heated, split, cooled, isolated use
- ½ Tbsp dried rosemary
- 1 Tbsp new spinach, steamed
- 1 (125 g) boneless, skinless chicken bosom, cooked
- ½ Tbsp fit salt, discretionary
- ½ Tbsp ground dark pepper

Procedure

1. Stock, milk, onion, two potatoes, and rosemary combining as one spot into the Vitamix holder in the request recorded and secure the top.
2. Start the blender with lower speed and afterward rapidly increment to its high speed.
3. Mix for 6 minutes, then, at that point lessen speed to Variable 3 and eliminate top attachment.
4. Add spinach, one potato, chicken, salt, and pepper through the top attachment opening and afterward mixing 30 second.

Butternut Squash Soup

Ingredients

- 1 Tbsp slashed new wise
- ½ Tbsp minced new rosemary
- 1 Tbsp ground new ginger
- 3 to 4 cups vegetable stock Newly ground dark pepper
-
- 2 Tbsp olive oil
- 1 enormous yellow onion, hacked
- ½ Tbsp ocean salt

- 1 (3-pound) butternut squash, stripped, cultivated, and cubed
- 3 garlic cloves, slashed
-

For serving

-
- Slashed parsley
- Toasted pepitas
- Dry bread

Procedure

1. Warmth the oil in an enormous pot over medium warmth. Then, at that point add the onion, salt, and a few toils of new pepper and sauté 5 to 8 minutes until delicate. Add the squash and cook to mollify, mixing sporadically, for 8 to 10 minutes.
2. Garlic, sage, rosemary, and ginger add and mix and cook 30 seconds to 1 moment, until fragrant, then, at that point, 3 cups of the stock add. Heat to the point of boiling, cover, and diminish warmth to a stew. Cook until the squash is delicate, 20 to 30 minutes. When bring to bubble, diminish warmth and cook 20-30 moment until squashis delicate.
3. Let cool marginally, mixing soup until smooth.If your soup is excessively thick, amount to 1 cup more stock and mix. Season to taste and present with parsley, pepitas, and dried up bread.

Vietnamese Noodle Bowl

Total time 45 min.

Ingredients

- 3 cups cooked chicken
- 1 Tbsp fish sauce
- 1 Tbsp shellfish sauce
- 1 Tbsp light soy sauce
- 200 gm egg noodles
- 2 ¼ cups snap pea

- 2 Tbsp sesame oil
- 2 carrots
- ¾ inch new ginger
- 3 scallions

Procedure

1. Cook the noodles appropriately. Extinguish and channel well.
2. Blanche the mange promote in bubbling salt water for around 2 min. Extinguish, channel well and cut down the middle slantingly.
3. The carrots, ginger and spring onions in warmed oil in a wok and fry. Add the noodles and the meat, fry for a couple of moments and season with the fish sauce, shellfish sauce and soy sauce. Season with pepper and serve.

Carrot Ginger Tofu Soup

Total Time : 25 Minutes

Ingredients

- 240 g carrots, divided
- ¼ medium onion, slashed
- 2 little garlic cloves, stripped
- 2 Tbsp olive oil
- ½ Tbsp salt

- ⅛ Tbsp ground white pepper
- 1 Tbsp new ginger root
- ⅓ cup light luxurious tofu
- 2 cups low sodium vegetable stock, stock

Procedure

- Carrots, onion and garlic place into the Vitamix holder and secure cover.
- Mix for 10 seconds, or until slashed.
- Warmth oil in a little skillet and sauté hacked fixings until onion is clear and carrots are delicate and add a little stock
- Remaining fixings Place into the Vitamix holder and afterward add sautéed fixings and secure top.
- At long last, mixing with fast for 3-4 moment.

Cuban Bean and Potato Soup

Total Time : 32 Minutes

Ingredients

- ½ Tbsp dried oregano
- ¼ Tbsp salt, discretionary
- 4 cups (960 ml) vegetable stock

- 3½ cup (730 g) dark beans, cooked, washed, depleted, isolated use
- 1½ little (140 g) potatoes, prepared, isolated use
- 1 Tbsp olive oil
- ½ medium onion, stripped, cleaved
- ½ huge (80 g) red ringer pepper, stemmed, cultivated, hacked
- ½ huge (80g) green ringer pepper, stemmed, cultivated, hacked
- 3 little garlic cloves, stripped
- 1 Tbsp white wine vinegar
- 1½ Tbsp ground cumin
- 1 dried sound leaf

Procedure

1. Warmed olive oil with medium-high then, at that point add onions, peppers, and garlic and cook for 8-10 moment.
2. Deglaze the container with vinegar and add the cumin, dried narrows leaf, oregano, and salt. Toasting the flavors and covering the vegetables with them, and afterward cook for 1 moment.
3. Vegetable stock, 3 cups dark beans, and sautéed vegetable blend place into the Vitamix holder in the request recorded and secure the cover.
4. Start the blender lower speed the speed up with high velocity and mixing brief 30 second.
5. Diminish speed and add 1 (100g) potato to the holder and the again mixing 30 seconds

Broccoli Cheese Soup

Total Time : 40 minutes

Ingredients

- ½ cup margarine
- 1 onion, slashed
- 450 gm frozen slashed broccoli
- 430 gm chicken stock

- 453 gm daydreams handled cheddar food, cubed
- 2 cups milk
- 1 Tbsp garlic powder
- ⅔ cup cornstarch
- 1 cup water

Procedure

- Liquefy spread with medium warmth and cook onion in margarine until mollified. Mix in broccoli, and cover with chicken stock. Broccoli cook 10 to 15 minutes.
- Lessen warmth, and mix in cheddar 3D squares until dissolved, then, at that point blend in milk and garlic powder.
- Mix cornstarch In a little bowl into water until disintegrated. Mix into soup cook, mixing oftentimes, until thick.

.

Cashew Cream of Mushroom

Total Time: 4 hour

Ingredients

- 2 Tbsp olive oil
- 2 (275 g) medium yellow onion, peeled, cut into large chunks

- 1½ pound mixed mushrooms, cleaned, halved
- 4 sprigs fresh thyme leaves
- kosher salt, to taste
- 1½ cup (200 g) raw cashews
- 6 cups (1.4 l) Vegetable Stock

Procedure

1. Heat a medium-high add olive oil, onions, mushrooms, thyme and salt. Saute for 10-12 minutes until mushrooms are soft and onions are translucent. Add cashews and saute for an additional 2 minutes.
2. Add vegetable, simmer in medium-low heat for 60-90 minutes.
3. Place the immersion blender into the middle of the stockpot and start the blender with a lower speed and then increase with high speed. Blending 1 minute then serve immediately, or cool in an ice bath and store in an airtight container in the refrigerator.

Thyme for Tomato Soup

Total Time: 21 minutes

Ingredients

- 1½ cup water
- 420 gm plum tomatoes
- 2 medium roma tomatoes
- 1 medium carrot
- 70 g sun-dried tomatoes
- 1½ Tbsp onion
- 1 little garlic clove
- 1½ Tbsp new thyme leaves

- 1 branch new oregano
- 1 Tbsp tomato glue
- ½ vegetable bouillon shape
- ½ Tbsp flax feast
- ½ cup almond milk

Procedure

1. All fixings place into the cleaning Vitamix holder in the request recorded and secure the top.
2. Start the blender with lower speed and afterward speed up.
3. Mix for 6 minutes until smooth

Beet Tomato and Macadamia Nut Soup

Total Time: 22 minutes

Ingredients

- ¾ cup water
- 240 g Roma tomato
- 2 (180 g) little beet, cooked
- 1 Tbsp ground cumin
- ½ vegetable bouillon shape
- ¼ cup macadamia nuts
- 1 Tbsp olive oil

Procedure

1. All fixings place into the cleaning Vitamix holder in the request recorded and secure the cover.
2. Start the blender with lower speed and afterward speed up.
3. Mix for 6 minutes until smooth

French Onion and Wild Mushroom Soup

Total Time: 21 minutes

Ingredients

- 3 medium onions, julienned
- 2 Tbsp olive oil
- 1 dried narrows leaf
- ½ Tbsp thyme leaves
- ½ Tbsp salt, discretionary
- ½Tbsp ground dark pepper
- 4 Tbsp unsalted margarine, or discretionary

- ½ ounce dry sherry, partitioned
- 4 cups hamburger stock, or cooked vegetable stock
- ½ ounce dried mushrooms
- 1 medium carrot
- 3 Tbsp chia seeds

Procedure

1. Add oil, onion, and narrows leaf and sauté container over medium-low warmth until brilliant earthy colored then, at that point add spread and preparing.
2. Deglaze with 80 ml of sherry and let decrease.
3. Then, at that point dried mushrooms, carrots, and chia seeds to the Vitamix compartment and secure the top. Start the blender with a lower speed and afterward increment with a high velocity.
4. Mix for 6 minutes until smooth
5. Add sautéed onion and remaining sherry and Blend for 20 seconds.

Apple Acorn Squash Soup

Total Time: 22 minutes

Ingredients

- 3 cups oak seed squash, stripped, cultivated, and cut into 1" blocks
- 1 Tbsp olive oil
- ½ little onion, stripped

- 1 garlic clove, stripped
- ½ medium apple, cored
- ¼ Tbsp dried thyme
- ⅛ Tbsp salt, discretionary
- 2 cups low sodium vegetable stock, stock

Procedure

1. Steam squash in a liner or microwave until fork delicate. Sauté onion and garlic in oil until onion is clear and delicate.
2. All fixings place into the cleaning Vitamix holder in the request recorded and secure the cover.
3. Start the blender with lower speed and afterward speed up and blend for 3-5 minutes until smooth

Acorn Squash and Turmeric Soup

Total Time: 15 minutes

Ingredients

- 4 cups (550 g) oak seed squash, cooked, stripped, cultivated
- 4 cups (960 ml) chicken stock, or vegetable stock
- 1 Tablespoon green curry glue
- 1 teaspoon ground turmeric
- ½ teaspoon salt, discretionary

- ¼ teaspoon ground dark pepper

Procedure

1. All fixings place into the cleaning Vitamix holder in the request recorded and secure the cover.
2. Start the blender with lower speed and afterward speed up.
3. Mix for 5 minutes 45 second until smooth

Cauliflower Mushroom Soup

Total Time: 45 minutes

Ingredients

- 1 medium white onion, slashed
- 8oz. (227g) mushrooms, white, cut (4 cups sliced)*
- 2 garlic cloves, minced
- 2-4 new thyme branches

- 2 Tbsp olive oil
- 1 cauliflower head, cut up in more modest pieces
- 4 cups natural vegetable stock
- 1/2 cup coconut cream***
- 1/2 Tbsp ocean salt
- 1/4 Tbsp newly ground pepper
- 1/8 Tbsp red pepper chips

Procedure

Consolidate the oil, onion, mushrooms, garlic, thyme, and olive oil join and blend In a Dutch broiler or enormous soup pot. Cook and mixing, 8-10 minutes. The cauliflower, vegetable stock, coconut cream add and bring to bubble. Decrease warmth and stew for 20 minutes then, at that point, move the soup to a fast blender until smooth. Return the soup to the pot, season with salt, pepper and red pepper drops, mix and taste. Change preparing if necessary. Keep warm on the most minimal setting until prepared to serve.Garnish and appreciate!

Cool Cucumber Soup

Total Time: 5 minutes

Ingredients

- 1 pound cucumbers , stripped and generally hacked
- ⅓ cup sharp cream
- ¼ cup new mint leaves
- 1 Tbsp rice vinegar
- fit salt

- cayenne pepper

Procedure

- All fixings place into the cleaning Vitamix holder in the request recorded and secure the top.
- Start the blender with lower speed and afterward speed up.
- Mix until smooth and afterward Serve chilled (prepared with salt and pepper), joined by bread and cheddar, whenever wanted.

Chocolate Almond Mousse

Total Time: 40 minutes

Ingredients

- ¼ Tbsp almond
- ½ Tbsp vanilla concentrate
- ¾ Tbsp Sweet'N Low® zero calorie sugar
- 1-ounce semi-sweet preparing chocolate, grated*
- 3 Tbsp unsweetened cocoa powder

- 2 cups substantial cream
- ½ ounce mixed chocolate, shaved for decorate

Procedure

1. All fixings consolidate in medium bowl and whip utilizing electric blender until delicate pinnacles Form. Then, at that point spoon into 4 Martini glasses and chill for no less than 30 minutes prior to serving. Trimming with shaved chocolate, whenever wanted.
2. To decrease sugars considerably further, substitute 1 ounce unsweetened preparing chocolate for semi-sweet heating chocolate and increment Sweet'N Low® zero calorie sugar to 2 Tbsp.

Strawberry Watermelon Smoothie Recipe

Total Time: 5 minutes

Ingredients

- 6 enormous mint leaves, new
- 2 Tbsp agave nectar, nectar
- 4 cups watermelon, diced, seedless
- 4 cups strawberries, frozen
- 2 Tbsp lime juice

Procedure

1. All fixings place into the cleaning Vitamix holder in the request recorded and secure the cover.
2. Start the blender with lower speed and afterward speed up.
3. Mix 30-60 second until smooth

Miso Lemon Tahini Dressing Recipe

Total Time: 5 minutes

Ingredients

- juice of 1/2 lemons
- dark pepper
- 1/4-1/2 cup water

- 1/2 cup tahini
- 2 Tbsp white miso

Procedure

1. The tahini, miso, lemon squeeze and dark pepper in a bowl, combine as one until smooth.
2. 1/4 cup of water add and mix well. For a runnier consistency, keep on adding water until the dressing arrives at the consistency you want.
3. Serve over rice, vegetables, beans

Homemade Orange Julius Recipe

Total Time: 10 minutes

Ingredients

- 340 gm Frozen Orange Juice Concentrate
- 2 cups Ice
- 1 cup Milk

- 1 cup Water
- ½ Tbsp Vanilla Extract
- ½ cup Sugar

Procedure

1. The milk, water, vanilla concentrate, sugar and squeezed orange concentrate add to a blender and mix until very much blended.
2. Then, at that point add the ice and again mix until smooth.
3. Fill singular clean glasses and present with a straw. Appreciate it

Raspberry Peach Cottage Cheese Smoothie Recipe

Total Time: 5 minutes

Ingredients

- 1/2 cup Frozen Raspberries
- Nectar, to taste
- run Cinnamon
- 1 cup Milk
- 1/2 cup Cottage Cheese
- 1 cup Frozen Peaches

Procedure

1. All fixings place into the cleaning Vitamix compartment in the request recorded and secure the cover.
2. Start the blender with lower speed and afterward speed up.
3. Mix until smooth

Strawberry Primm's Slush Recipe

Total Time: 5 minutes

Ingredients

- 16 ounces Frozen Strawberries
- 1 cup Pimm's No.1 Liqueur
- 3/4 cup Lemon Lime Soda
- 1 Lemon, squeezed

Procedure

1. The frozen strawberries, Pimm's, pop and lemon juice place in a mix and afterward until the strawberries are puréed.
2. Pour in a medium pitcher or split between 4 glasses, and afterward embellish with a strawberry half and branches of mint prior to serving.

Basil Peach Agua Fresca Recipe

Total Time: 10 minutes

Ingredients

- 6 Peaches, Pitted
- juice of one Lemon
- 2 1/2 cups Cold Water
- 2 small bunches Fresh Basil Leaves
- Ice Cubes

Procedure

1. Mix the peaches into a smooth purée and promptly blend in with the lemon juice.
2. Consolidate the peach purée in an enormous container with the water, basil, and afterward ice blocks, and serve right away.

Butternut Squash Bisque Recipe

Total Time: 1 hour

Ingredients

- 1 Tbsp canola oil
- 1 Tbsp unsalted margarine
- ½ cup diced onion
- ¾ cup diced carrots
- 4 cups stripped and cubed butternut squash
- 3 cups vegetable stock
- salt and ground dark pepper to taste
- ground nutmeg
- ½ cup weighty cream

Procedure

1. Warmth the oil and soften the margarine and cook and mix the onion in the spread and oil under the delicate.
2. Carrots and squash, blend them into the pot. Pour in vegetable stock, and season with salt, pepper, and nutmeg, and afterward heat to the point of boiling, lessen warmth, and stew until vegetables are delicate.
3. In a blender, puree the soup combination until smooth. Get back to the pot, then, at that point mix in the weighty cream. Warmth through, however don't bubble. Serve warm with a scramble of nutmeg.

Gingerbread Eggnog Recipe

Total Time: 5 minutes

Procedure

- 2 tbsp Molasses, in addition to additional for showering
- Squeeze ground ginger
- Whipped cream, for fixing Ice
- 1 tbsp Cinnamon sugar
- 1 cup eggnog
- 1 cup vodka
- 1 cup Kahlúa

Procedure

1. Four mixed drink glasses and dunk in cinnamon sugar wet edges.
2. In a mixed drink shaker loaded up with ice, add eggnog, vodka, Kahlúa, molasses, and ginger and shake to blending and join well.
3. Fill rimmed glasses. Top with whipped cream and afterward shower with molasses prior to serving.

Rumchata Chai Latte Recipe

Total Time: 15 minutes

Ingredients

- 1/2 Tbsp Ground Cloves
- 1/2Tbsp Cardamom
- 1/2 Tbsp Nutmeg

- 1/4 Tbsp White Pepper
- 1 cup Instant Tea
- 1/4 cups Granulated Sugar
- 1 Tbsp Ground Ginger
- 1 Tbsp Cinnamon

Procedure

1. To make the Chai Mix:
2. Every one of the dry fixings In a huge bowl, join well .
3. Spot in a blender and mixing until a fine powder structures.
4. Keep put away in a container
5. To make the Rumchata Chai Latte:
6. Spot 2Tbsp of chai blend into a 10-ounce mug.
7. Fill most of the way with bubbling water and afterward mix until disintegrated. Fill the rest with the way with Rumchata.

Pumpkin Pie Ice Cream Shooters Recipe

Total Time: 10 minutes

Ingredients

- 1/2 cup Graham Cracker Crumbs
- Whipped Cream, For serving
- 2 cups Pumpkin Ice Cream

- 2 cups Milk

Procedure

1. Draw apparition faces white paper cups with dark marker
2. The frozen yogurt and milk add into a blender and mix until smooth.
3. Empty the milkshakes into minimal shot glasses and top with whipped cream and afterward a tidying of graham wafer morsels. Serve!

Blender Tortilla Soup Recipe

Total Time: 15 minutes

Ingredients

- 2 cups high temp Water

- 1 15 ounce can Corn, Drained
- 1 15 oz can Black Beans, Drained and washed
- 1/2 cups Cooked Chicken, Diced
- Extra Cilantro and Avocado for Serving
- Tortilla Chips
- 2 cup Diced Tomatoes, Undrained
- 1 huge Carrot
- 1/2 medium Red Bell Pepper, Seeds eliminated
- 1/2 huge Ripe Avocado
- 2-3 twigs Fresh Cilantro
- 1 Tbsp No-Salt Herb Seasoning
- 3/4 Tbsp Salt
- 3/4 Tbsp Garlic Powder
- 1/4 Tbsp Onion Powder

Procedure

1. The tomatoes, carrot, chime pepper, avocado, cilantro, spice preparing, salt, garlic powder, onion powder, and water add a blender and mixing until totally smooth. Taste and change flavors on a case by case basis.
2. The corn, dark beans, and chicken and heartbeat again blandeing
3. Serve the soup with disintegrated tortilla chips.
4. Cilantro and avocado put on top of it

Banana Smoothie Recipe

Total: 5 minutes

INGREDIENTS

- 1 cup unsweetened plain almond milk
- 1 Tbsp vanilla concentrate

- 2 cups frozen cut bananas
- 1/2 cup non-fat plain Greek yogurt
- 1/2 Tbsp ground flax seeds

Directions

- All fixings place in a reasonable blender. Blender start with a high velocity blender and mix on high until smooth. Alternative to add more almond milk depending on the situation.

Mixed Berry Smoothie

Total Time 6 minutes

INGREDIENTS

- 1/2 cups frozen blended berries
- 3/4 cup vanilla Greek yogurt
- 1 Tbsp nectar
- 1/2 cups squeezed apple can likewise utilize almond milk, skim milk, coconut milk or other kind of juice
- 1 banana cut
- Enhancement: new berries and mint twigs

INSTRUCTIONS

1. Squeezed apple, banana, berries, and yogurt Place them in an unmistakable blender. Mixing until smooth. Smoothie appears too thick and afterward add somewhat more fluid (1/4 cup).
2. To get more taste and add nectar. Topping with new berries and mint branches

Spinach Smoothie Recipe

Total Time10 mins

Ingredients

- 2 cups child spinach
- ½ cup non-fat plain Greek yogurt
- 1 cup unsweetened almond milk
- 1 cup ice blocks
- 2 cups frozen pineapple lumps
- ½ cup frozen banana cuts, around 1 medium banana
- 1 cup diced apple

Instructions

1. Ice blocks, pineapple, banana cuts, diced apple, child spinach, yogurt, and almond milk combining as one and afterward place in the blender.
2. Cover and blender start with medium speed for around 30 seconds and afterward utilizing the alter depending on the situation. From that point forward, blender Increase to rapid for 15 to 30 seconds until thick and smooth.
3. Add more almond milk

Peanut Butter Smoothie Recipe

Prep:5 mins

Ingredients

- Spot of nutmeg
- Little modest bunch, ice 3D squares
- 1 cups oat milk
- 1 banana, stripped and cleaved
- 20g peanut butter
- 1 tbsp moved oats
- Spot of cinnamon
- spot of allspice

Method

- Every one of the fixings combining as one, place in a blender until smooth. Then, at that point fill a tall glass, organize pleasantly.

Blueberry Smoothie Recipe

Total:
5 mins

Ingredients

- 2 Tbsp white sugar
- ½ Tbsp vanilla concentrate
- ⅛ Tbsp ground nutmeg
- 1 cup blueberries (frozen or new)
- 1 cup holder plain yogurt
- ¾ cup 2% diminished fat milk

Directions

1. Mix the blueberries, yogurt, milk, sugar, vanilla, and nutmeg combining as one spot in a blender until foamy, and afterward scratching down the sides of the blender with a spatula periodically. Serve pleasantly.

Mango Smoothie Recipes

TOTAL TIME: 3 mins

INGREDIENTS

- 2 new mangoes
- 1 frozen banana, can utilize thawed if utilizing frozen mango
- 1/2 cup milk, dairy
- 1/2 cup yogurt, dairy

INSTRUCTIONS

- Frozen mango and a frozen banana blending place in a blender . Blender start with gradually and afterward speed up until mixed without a hitch.
- Pour smoothies in an artisan container and afterward utilize either a treated steel straw

Kale Smoothie Recipe

Prep:5 mins

Ingredient

- enormous modest bunch frozen pineapple lumps
- medium-sized lump ginger
- 1 Tbsp cashew nuts
- 1 banana
- 2 modest bunches kale
- ½ avocado
- ½ lime, squeeze as it were

Instructions

Every one of the fixings blending and spot into solid smoothie producer and afterward add an enormous sprinkle of water and barrage. At long last, add more water until you have the ideal consistency and present with pleasantly.

Vanilla Protein Smoothie Recipe

Prep Time: 5 minutes

Ingredients

- ½ Tbsp vanilla concentrate
- 1 cup frozen pineapple
- 1 banana
- 2 Tbsp peanut butter
- ½ cup Greek yogurt
- ½ cup milk
- 8 ice blocks
- Enhancement: we utilized toasted coconut and new raspberries

Instructions

1. All fixings, breaking the bananas, combining as one into blender. Mixing until smooth.
2. Serve quickly and afterward store in a shrouded container in the fridge for 2 days.

Cinnamon Apple Smoothie

Prep Time: 5 minutes

Ingredients

- ½ Tbsp vanilla concentrate
- ¼ Tbsp cinnamon
- 2 cups new apple pieces
- 1 ready banana
- ½ cup Greek yogurt
- ¼ cup milk
- 8 ice 3D shapes

Instructions

1. Apple cut into little pieces . Spot all fixings combining as one, place into in a blender, breaking the banana into pieces. Then, at that point Blending until smooth and foamy, pausing and scratching down the sides as fundamental. Topping with an apple cut. Serve and store in a shrouded container in the fridge for 1 day.

Carrot Smoothie Recipe

Total:
35 mins

Ingredients

- 1 ½ cups ice shapes
- 3 (1 inch) pieces Orange strip twists
- 1 cup cut carrots
- ½ Tbsp finely destroyed orange strip
- 1 cup squeezed orange

Directions

1. Initially, carrots cook bubbling in a covered little pan around 15 moment until delicate . Channel and cool well.
2. After that the carrots, place in a blender, add finely destroyed orange strip and squeezed orange. Then, at that point mixing until smooth and afterward add ice 3D squares, again mixing .
3. at long last, fill glasses. Whenever wanted , decorate with orange strip twists.

Peach Smoothie Recipe

Total Time 6 minutes

INGREDIENTS

- 1/2 cup frozen mango
- 3/4 cup vanilla Greek yogurt
- new peaches and mint branches for embellish
- 1/2 cups peach nectar
- 1 banana divided
- 1/2 cups frozen peaches

INSTRUCTIONS

1. All fixings blending and spot in an unmistakable blender
2. Mix until smooth.
3. Fill 2 glasses and enhancement with new peaches and mint twigs whenever wanted and serve pleasantly.

Grape Smoothie

Prep Time: 5 minutes

Ingredients

- 2 cups seedless red grapes
- 1 banana
- ½ cup milk
- ½ cup Greek yogur

Instructions

1. Prior to beginning the formula, make sure to hold up the grapes!
2. All fixings blending and spot in the blender, beginning with the milk and yogurt, breaking the banana into pieces. Mix until smooth and afterward adding a sprinkle more fluid as important to go to the ideal consistency.

Acai-Peanut Protein Shake

INGREDIENTS

- 1 3.5-ounce bundle frozen unsweetened açaí purée
- 1 cup almond milk
- ⅓ cup frozen strawberries
- 2 cup vanilla whey protein powder
- Tbsp regular peanut butter

Instructions

1. All fixings combining as one into blender. Mixing until smooth.
2. Serve right away

CBD Mango Smoothie

Total Time 10 minutes

Ingredients

- 1/2 tbsp ground turmeric
- 1/2 tbsp NUHEALTH CBD Hemp Oil
- Touch of genuine salt
- 1 cup of ice
- 1/2 cup of frozen mango
- 1/2 frozen banana, cleaved
- 1-inch piece of ginger, stripped, finely ground
- 1/2 cup unsweetened coconut water

Instructions

1. All fixings combining as one into blender. Mixing until smooth.
2. Serve promptly and appreciate!

Mango, Berry & Banana Smoothie

INGREDIENTS

- 3/4 cup coconut water
- 1/2 cup frozen blackberries or blueberries
- 1/4 cup plain yogurt
- 1 Tbsp ground flaxseeds
- 1 exceptionally ready stripped banana
- 2 pitted Medjool dates
- 1 cup frozen mango pieces

PREPARATION

1. All fixings combining as one into blender. Mixing until smooth.
2. Serve promptly and appreciate!

Green Peanut Butter Smoothie

Ingredient

- 1 banana
- 1 cup nut milk
- 1 cup torn kale
- 2 tablespoons peanut butter
- ¼ teaspoon ground cinnamon

Instructions

1. All fixings combining as one into blender. Mixing until smooth.
2. Serve quickly and appreciate!

Banana Almond Smoothie

INGREDIENTS

- 1 frozen stripped banana, broken into 3–4 pieces
- 1 cup almond milk
- 1 Tbsp almond spread
- 1/8 Tbsp almond extricate

Instructions

1. All fixings combining as one into blender.
2. The blender start gradually then speed up and afterward mixing until smooth.
3. Serve promptly and appreciate!

Blueberry-Chia Smoothie

TOTAL TIME 5 mins

INGREDIENTS

- ½ cup milk
- ½ cup Greek yogurt
- 1 cup blueberries , frozen
- 1 banana
- 1 Tbsp chia seeds
- 1 Tbsp Ceylon Cinnamon
- nectar

INSTRUCTIONS

1. All fixings, place in the blender.
2. The blender start gradually then speed up and afterward mixing until smooth.
3. Add somewhat more fluid – milk or water, and Blend once more.
4. Taste the smoothie and add extra sugar
5. Move the smoothie into a smoothie glass.
6. Serve and appreciate!

Blackberry and Yogurt Breakfast Smoothie

TOTAL TIME
10 MINUTES

INGREDIENTS

- 1/2 cup new squeezed orange
- 1 Tbsp finely ground stripped ginger
- 1 Tbsp nectar or light agave syrup
- 1 banana
- 2 cups (pressed) spinach leaves
- 1 cup frozen blackberries
- 1 cup nonfat yogurt

Planning

1. All fixings combining as one into blender.
2. The blender start gradually then speed up and afterward mixing until smooth.
3. Serve quickly and appreciate!

Blueberry Peanut Butter Protein Smoothie

TOTAL TIME
5 minutes

Ingredients

- 1 scoop peanut butter protein powder
- 1/2-1 cup without dairy milk of decision
- 1 Tbsp seed cycling blend
- 1 ready banana, recently cut and frozen
- 1/2 cup frozen wild blueberries
- 1 huge modest bunch natural spinach

Instructions

1. All fixings combining as one into blender.
2. The blender start gradually then increse with rapid and afterward Blending until smooth
3. Taste and change flavor on a case by case basis, adding more banana for pleasantness, and add more sans dairy milk on a case by case basis to thin.
4. Serve and appreciate right away.

Creamy Carrot Cake Smoothies

TOTAL TIME
5 minutes

Ingredients

- 1 tsp new minced or ground ginger
- 1 sound squeeze ground nutmeg
- 1/2 – 1 cup without dairy milk
- 1 scoop plain or vanilla protein powder
- 1 huge ready frozen banana
- 1 little carrot, hacked
- 1 pitted date
- 1/4 tbsp ground cinnamon
- 1/2 tbsp vanilla concentrate

Instructions

1. Banana, carrot, date , cinnamon, vanilla, new ginger, nutmeg, without dairy milk , and protein powder place in blender and afterward to a rapid blender and mix until rich and smooth. Add more without dairy milk depending on the situation to thin/empower mixing.
2. Taste and change flavor on a case by case basis, adding more cinnamon for warmth, ginger for zest/kick, or date for pleasantness.
3. Fill in with no guarantees or trimming with destroyed carrot, destroyed coconut, or pecans or hemp seeds

Red Velvet Cake Smoothie

TOTAL TIME
5 minutes

Ingredients

- 2 ready, frozen (stripped) banana
- 1/3 cup cubed beet
- 2 Tbsp cocoa powder
- 2 pitted dates
- 3/4 cup dairy free milk
- 1/2 tbsp vanilla concentrate

Instructions

1. All fixings place into a rapid blender and mix until velvety and smooth and afterward adding more sans dairy milk depending on the situation to help mix.
2. Adding more dates for pleasantness, beets for an earthier flavor
3. Serve right away. Appreciate with no guarantees or top with red velvet cake balls, cocoa/cacao powder, beetroot powder.

Superfoods Green Lemonade Smoothie

TOTAL TIME
10 minutes

Ingredients

- 1 tsp baobab powder
- 1 tsp moringa powder
- 1 tsp spirulina
- 1 Tbsp hemp seeds
- 1/2 – 1 cup water to thin/help mix
- 1 little frozen ready banana
- 2 ½ cups frozen pineapple
- 1 inch handle ginger
- 1 medium lime or lemon, squeezed
- 1 little small bunch new spinach
- 3/4 cup coconut water
- 1/2 cup light coconut milk

Instructions

1. All fixings combining as one into a blender.
2. The blender begins gradually then speeds up and afterward mixing until smooth like as rich.
3. Adding more coconut milk for smoothness, pineapple or banana to thicken, lime or lemon for pungency, or ginger for punch.
4. Appreciate with no guarantees, or trimming with extra hemp seeds
5. Best when new. In the event that you have extras, freeze into popsicles or ice block molds. At the point when prepared to utilize, basically mix the smoothie ice 3D shapes in your blender with more coconut water and coconut milk.

Super Green Spirulina Smoothie

TOTAL TIME

5 minutes

Ingredients

- 1 medium ready banana
- 1/2 cup cut cucumber
- 3/4 - 1 cup light coconut milk
- 1 cup spinach or hacked kale
- 1 tsp spirulina powder
- 1 Tbsp hemp seed

Instructions

1. add frozen banana, cucumber, coconut milk, spinach, spirulina, and hemp seed place into clear blender and afterward mix until rich and smooth
2. To make dainty add water or coconut milk and to make thick ice or frozen banana
3. Adding more banana for pleasantness, cucumber for newness
4. Serve right away

Coconut Papaya Smoothie

TOTAL TIME

5 minutes

Ingredients

- 1/2 cup carrot juice
- 1/2 cup light coconut milk
- 1-2 Tbsp agave nectar
- 1/2 cups frozen ready papaya 3D squares
- 1 little ready banana
- 1-2 tbsp minced ginger
- 2 medium limes, squeezed

Instructions

1. Add all fixings to a blender and mix until rich and smooth, adding more carrot juice or coconut milk in the event that it experiences difficulty mixing.
2. Taste and change flavors on a case by case basis, adding more banana for pleasantness, lime for acridity
3. Appreciate right away.

Strawberry Chia Watermelon Smoothie

TOTAL TIME
5 minutes

Ingredients

- 1/2 - 3/4 cup unsweetened plain almond milk
- 1 medium lime
- 1 Tbsp chia or hemp seeds
- 1/2 cups new watermelon
- 1 cup frozen strawberries
- 1/2 medium ready banana

Instructions

1. Add all fixings to a blender and afterward mix until rich and smooth
2. Taste and change preparing on a case by case basis, adding more lime for corrosiveness, banana for pleasantness
3. To serve top with extra chia seeds to taunt watermelon seeds! Best when new, however extras save canvassed in the cooler for 1-2 days.

www.ingramcontent.com/pod-product-compliance
Ingram Content Group UK Ltd.
Pitfield, Milton Keynes, MK11 3LW, UK
UKHW022014190726
13853UKWH00005B/1937